DOGS SET V

Brittany Spaniels

Julie Murray
ABDO Publishing Company

APR   2005

Boulder City Library
701 Adams Boulevard
Boulder City, NV 89005

visit us at
www.abdopub.com

Published by ABDO Publishing Company, 4940 Viking Drive, Edina, Minnesota 55435. Copyright © 2003 by Abdo Consulting Group, Inc. International copyrights reserved in all countries. No part of this book may be reproduced in any form without written permission from the publisher.

Printed in the United States.

Cover Photo: Animals Animals
Interior Photos: Animals Animals pp. 7, 11, 17, 21; Corbis pp. 5, 9, 13, 15, 19

Contributing Editors: Kate A. Conley, Kristin Van Cleaf, Kristianne E. Vieregger
Art Direction & Graphics: Neil Klinepier

Library of Congress Cataloging-In-Publication Data

Murray, Julie, 1969-
    Brittany Spaniels / Julie Murray.
        p. cm. -- (Dogs Set V)
    Summary: An introduction to the physical characteristics, behavior, and proper care of Brittany Spaniels.
    Includes bibliographical references (p.).
    ISBN 1-57765-922-8
    1. Brittany spaniel--Juvenile literature. [1. Brittany spaniel. 2. Dogs.] I. Title.

SF429.B78 M87 2003
636.752'4--dc21

                                                                              2002074654

Contents

The Dog Family

Dogs and humans have been living together for thousands of years. Dogs were first tamed about 12,000 years ago. They were used as guards, hunters, and companions.

Today, about 400 different dog **breeds** exist. They can differ greatly in appearance. Some can weigh as much as 200 pounds (91 kg). Others are small enough to fit in the palms of your hands.

Despite these differences, all dogs belong to the same scientific **family**. It is called Canidae. The name comes from the Latin word *canis*, which means dog.

The Canidae family includes more than just **domestic** dogs. Foxes, jackals, coyotes, and wolves belong to the Canidae family, too. In fact, many people believe today's domestic dogs descended from wolves.

Brittanys have many of the same instincts as wolves.

Brittanys

Brittanys were first **bred** in the 1800s. They are one of Europe's oldest hunting breeds. Brittanys received their name from Brittany, France. It is the area where the breed began.

No one is exactly sure of the Brittany's history. Some people believe that Brittanys may be a cross between English setters and French spaniels.

The earliest record of a Brittany in the United States was in 1912. At that time, Brittanys were known as Brittany spaniels. Then in 1982, the **American Kennel Club (AKC)** dropped the word *spaniel* from the breed's name.

Today, these dogs are called Brittanys in the United States. But they are still known as Brittany spaniels in other parts of the world.

Brittanys have become a popular breed in the United States.

What They're Like

Brittanys are ideal hunting dogs. Their incredible tracking and retrieving skills make them great companions for hunters. They also have the **poise** to perform well in dog shows.

Brittanys are excellent pets for an active family, too. They are gentle, loving, and intelligent. And, Brittanys get along well with children and other pets.

In addition, Brittanys are easy to train and eager to please their owners. They should never be treated roughly, or they may become timid and shy. Brittanys need patient owners who will encourage proper behavior.

Though Brittanys make excellent hunting dogs, many families keep them just as pets.

Coat and Color

Like many other sporting dogs, the Brittany has a **dense** coat. This coat protects the dog from harsh weather.

A Brittany's coat has fine, flat hair. The hair can be straight or wavy. A Brittany also has feathery hair on the back of its legs. Its ears have some fringe on them.

A Brittany's coat may be orange and white, **liver** and white, or black and white. The Brittany's coat can also be a combination of any three of these colors. However, the **AKC** will not allow a Brittany with any black in its coat to compete in dog shows.

A Brittany's dark nose matches the color of its coat. This Brittany has an orange-and-white-colored coat.

Size

The Brittany is a medium-size dog. It can weigh between 30 and 40 pounds (14 and 18 kg). Its height can range from 17 to 21 inches (43 to 53 cm) at the shoulder.

The Brittany's body is compact. This **breed** has long, powerful legs. It also has a deep chest and a short, straight back. The back slopes down slightly from the dog's shoulders to its tail.

A Brittany's tail is usually **docked** to about four inches (10 cm) in length. But some Brittanys are born without a tail.

The Brittany has a round head with heavy eyebrows. They protect the dog's deep-set eyes. The Brittany's ears are set high on its head. They are short and slightly rounded at the tips.

A Brittany's tail is often kept short to prevent injuries while hunting.

Care

Grooming a Brittany is easy. Its coat needs to be brushed or combed about once a week. This will keep the coat clean and shiny. A Brittany sheds its coat twice a year. These are good times to have your Brittany professionally groomed.

A Brittany only needs a bath a few times a year. But your Brittany may become dirty from a hunting trip or playing in the yard. If so, it may need a bath more often.

Like any dog, the Brittany needs to visit the **veterinarian** at least once a year for a checkup. The veterinarian can check your dog for illnesses and give it shots to prevent diseases. If you are not going to **breed** your dog, have the veterinarian **spay** or **neuter** it.

Bathing your Brittany can be fun!

Feeding

Brittanys are active dogs, so they need well-balanced, nutritional meals. Their food can be dry, moist, or semimoist. Most dogs will eat a high-quality, dry dog food. Others prefer to have some canned food mixed in with their dry food.

Find a type of food your Brittany enjoys and stick with it. Changes in diet should be done gradually to prevent stomach problems. It is also important to give your dog fresh, clean water every day.

Brittanys enjoy chewing on rawhide bones, nylon bones, and cattle hooves. Dog biscuits are also good treats for Brittanys. But Brittanys need to be watched carefully with these special treats. They may eat too much or choke.

Brittany puppies often eat lots of food because they are growing quickly.

Things They Need

Brittanys need regular exercise. They need space to run and play. They love to go jogging or walking. They also enjoy playing fetch.

Regular exercise will keep Brittanys from becoming mischievous. It will also keep them healthy and strong. If you have an inactive lifestyle, a Brittany might not be the right dog for you.

Like all dogs, Brittanys need a quiet place in the house to rest. They also need something comfortable to lie on. A dog bed or soft blanket works well for this.

Every dog should wear a collar with two tags. One tag shows the dog has had its shots. The other tag shows the dog's name and its owner's address and phone number. A dog can also have a **tattoo** or **microchip** for identification.

With a healthy, active lifestyle, a Brittany may live to be 15 years old.

Puppies

Baby dogs are called puppies. A mother dog is **pregnant** for about nine weeks. Brittanys have about six to eight puppies in a **litter**.

Puppies are born blind and deaf. Their eyes and ears will begin working when they are about two weeks old. They can walk at three weeks, and they are usually **weaned** at about seven weeks of age.

Puppies can be given away or sold when they are about eight weeks old. If you are going to buy a **purebred** puppy, make sure to buy it from a qualified **breeder**. Many puppies and older dogs are also available from the **Humane Society**.

It is important to take your puppy to the **veterinarian**. He or she will give your puppy the shots it needs to stay healthy. A puppy should start getting its shots when it is between six and eight weeks old.

Puppies learn many important behaviors from their mother.

Glossary

American Kennel Club (AKC) - a club that studies, breeds, and exhibits purebred dogs.

breed - a group of dogs sharing the same appearance and characteristics. A breeder is a person who raises dogs. Raising dogs is often called breeding them.

dense - thick.

dock - to cut the tail to a shorter length.

domestic - living with humans.

family - a group that scientists use to classify similar plants and animals. It ranks above a genus and below an order.

Humane Society - an organization that cares for and protects animals.

litter - all the puppies born at one time to a mother dog.

liver - a grayish, reddish-brown color.

microchip - a small computer chip. A veterinarian inserts the chip between a dog's shoulder blades. If the dog is lost, the Humane Society can scan the chip to find the dog's identification information and owners.

neuter - to remove a male animal's reproductive parts.

poise - a calm, confident manner.

pregnant - having one or more babies growing within the body.

purebred - an animal whose parents are both from the same breed.

spay - to remove a female animal's reproductive parts.

tattoo - a permanent design made on the skin. An owner can have an identification number tattooed on the leg of his or her dog.

veterinarian - a doctor who cares for animals.

wean - to accustom an animal to eating food other than its mother's milk.

Web Sites

Would you like to learn more about Brittanys? Please visit our Web site at **www.abdopub.com** to find up-to-date Web site links about Brittanys, their qualities, and more. These links are routinely monitored and updated to provide the most current information available.

Index